THIS WALKER BOOK BELONGS TO:

_____

_____

_____

HONEY the yellow Labrador
and her puppies

The cat

JO-JO
the Jack Russell terrier

TAG
the Dalmatian

LITTLE PETE
the Yorkshire terrier

SUSIE
the West Highland terrier

BEN
the bulldog

DAISY
the dachshund

ROVER
the mongrel

MR. CHIPS
the black Labrador

HENRY
the Pekingese

WENDY
the other mongrel

To Leon Achilleos
P.H.

To Jimmy Wool
B.F.

First published 1993 by
Walker Books Ltd
87 Vauxhall Walk
London SE11 5HJ

This edition published 1996

2 4 6 8 10 9 7 5 3

Text © 1993 Peter Hansard
Illustrations © 1993 Barbara Firth

This book has been typeset in Bembo.

Printed in Hong Kong

British Library Cataloguing in Publication Data
A catalogue record for this book is
available from the British Library.

ISBN 0-7445-4736-9

WAG WAG WAG

or WHAT DOGS DO

Written by
Peter Hansard

Illustrated by
Barbara Firth

WALKER BOOKS
AND SUBSIDIARIES
LONDON · BOSTON · SYDNEY

sniff   sniff

roll   piddle

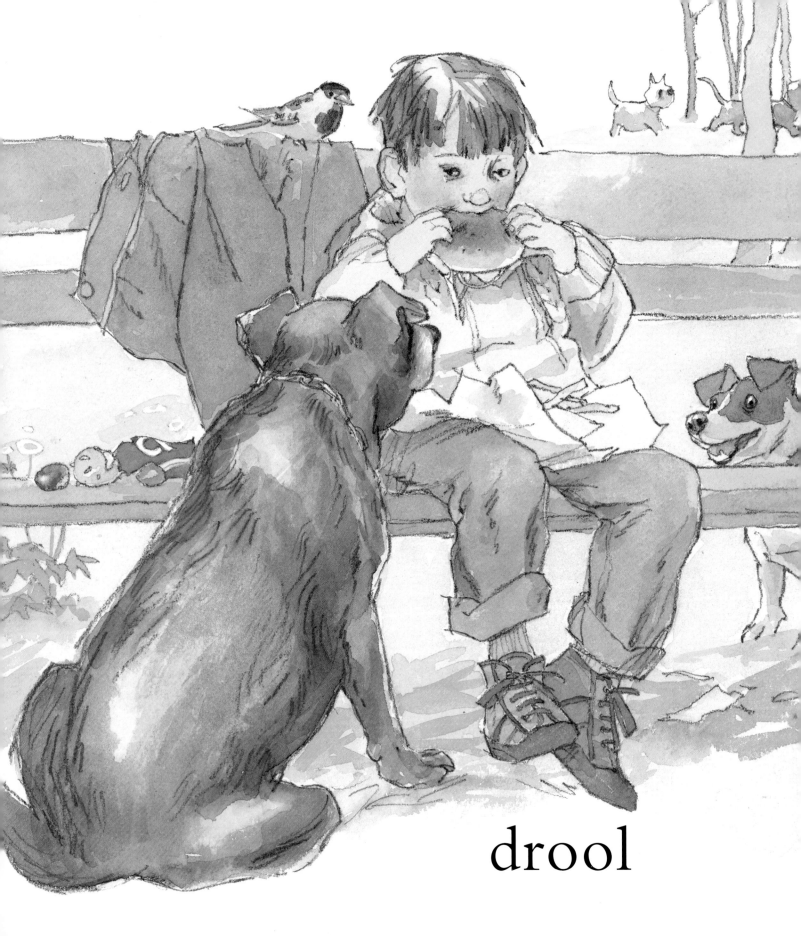

drool

dribble

woof

woof woof play ball

chase

race

pant

leap

splash   shake

dig   dig

scratch

scratch

scratch

walk   sit

yawn

tug

nip   chew

gobble   gobble

gnaw

sleep

snore

wag wag wag

HONEY the yellow Labrador
and her puppies

The cat

JO-JO
the Jack Russell terrier

TAG
the Dalmatian

LITTLE PETE
the Yorkshire terrier

SUSIE
the West Highland terrier

BEN
the bulldog

DAISY
the dachshund

ROVER
the mongrel

MR. CHIPS
the black Labrador

HENRY
the Pekingese

WENDY
the other mongrel

MORE WALKER PAPERBACKS
For You to Enjoy

Also illustrated by Barbara Firth

"QUACK!" SAID THE BILLY-GOAT
by Charles Causley

The animals all go crazy, when the farmer lays an egg!

"Very attractive … very funny." *Parents*

0-7445-5246-X   £4.99

WE LOVE THEM
by Martin Waddell

Two children love their pet dog, Ben. But he's growing old…

"Introduces death naturally and matter-of-factly …
will bear repeated readings." *Susan Hill, The Sunday Times*

0-7445-1774-5   £4.50

CAN'T YOU SLEEP, LITTLE BEAR?
by Martin Waddell

Winner of the Smarties Book Prize and the Kate Greenaway Medal

"The most perfect children's book ever written or illustrated…
It evaporates and dispels all fear of the dark." *Molly Keane, The Sunday Times*

0-7445-1316-2   £4.99

THE PARK IN THE DARK
by Martin Waddell

Winner of the Kurt Maschler Award

The night-time adventures of three soft-toy animals.

"Absolutely wonderful. The perfect picture book." *Chris Powling, BBC Radio*

0-7445-1740-0   £4.99

Walker Paperbacks are available from most booksellers, or by post from B.B.C.S., P.O. Box 941, Hull, North Humberside HU1 3YQ
24 hour telephone credit card line 01482 224626
To order, send: Title, author, ISBN number and price for each book ordered, your full name and address,
cheque or postal order payable to BBCS for the total amount and allow the following for postage and packing:
UK and BFPO: £1.00 for the first book, and 50p for each additional book to a maximum of £3.50.
Overseas and Eire: £2.00 for the first book, £1.00 for the second and 50p for each additional book.
Prices and availability are subject to change without notice.